BRANCH LINE TO MINEHEAD

Vic Mitchell and Keith Smith

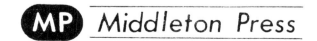

MP Middleton Press

First published July 1990

ISBN 0 906520 80 0

© Middleton Press 1990

Design and Laser typesetting -
Deborah Goodridge
Barbara Mitchell

Published by Middleton Press
Easebourne Lane
Midhurst, West Sussex
GU29 9AZ
Tel. (0730) 813169

Printed & bound by Biddles Ltd,
Guildford and Kings Lynn

CONTENTS

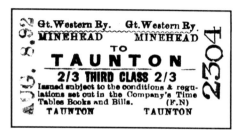

ACKNOWLEDGEMENTS

We are grateful to many of those mentioned in the captions for the assistance received and also to D.Bishop, Dr.P.Cattermole, G.Croughton, N.Langridge, E.Staff, G.Stagg, N.Stanyon, C. van den Arend and J.A.M. Vaughan.   As always our wives have been of immeasurable help.

The authors and publishers regret that they are not able to supply copies of pictures contained in their publications, but requests for prints of photographs from the Mowat Collection can be made to W.R.Burton, 3 Fairway, Clifton, York and those marked Lens of Sutton can be obtained from 4 Westmead Road, Sutton, Surrey.

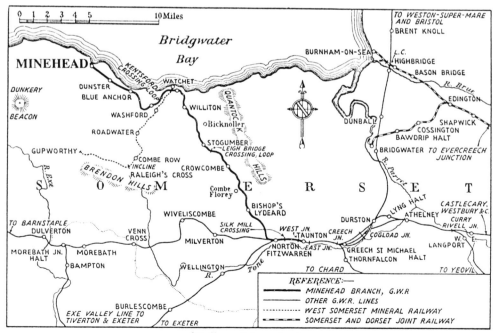

(Railway Magazine)

HISTORICAL BACKGROUND

The broad gauge track of the Bristol & Exeter Railway spread steadily west, arriving at Taunton on 1st July 1842, and being extended through to Exeter on 1st May 1844. A branch north to Watchet was opened on 31st March 1862, although a station at the junction at Norton Fitzwarren was not provided until 1873. A branch to Barnstaple from this junction was opened on 6th August 1871. The Watchet line was built by the West Somerset Railway Co. following its Act of 17th August 1857. It was laid to the broad gauge of 7ft.0¼ins. and was operated by the B&ER.

The Minehead Railway Co. obtained an Act in 1870 to extend the branch to Minehead, the line being opened on 16th July 1874. The train service was also provided by the B&ER.

The main lines through Taunton were fitted with a third rail in 1876, to allow for the working of standard gauge trains. The Minehead branch was converted from broad to standard gauge between 28th and 30th October 1882. The B&ER was absorbed into the Great Western Railway in 1876, but the WSR remained an independent company until 1897 and the Minehead Railway until 1922, although the GWR operated the branch.

In order to reduce congestion in the Taunton area, the GWR embarked on a scheme in 1930 to quadruple the running lines through the station and for about two miles east and west of it. Improvements to the branch followed in 1934 when two passing loops were added and the Blue Anchor - Minehead section was doubled. In 1936, the Norton Fitzwarren - Bishops Lydeard length was also doubled.

Apart from the war years, heavy holiday traffic was handled until the mid-1960s. To reduce operating losses, diesel multiple units were introduced on 10th September 1962 and tickets were issued on the trains from 26th February 1968, although only to passengers from intermediate stations. After prolonged protestations, the branch closed on 4th January 1971.

On 5th May 1971, a new West Somerset Railway Co. was incorporated. In 1975 it obtained a lease for the branch from the Somerset

GEOGRAPHICAL SETTING

Taunton is situated between the Quantock and Blackdown Hills, on the Alluvium of the River Tone. At Norton Fitzwarren the branch follows a tributary of the Tone towards Bishops Lydeard, north of which it climbs onto a much faulted area composed of Mercia Mudstones, Budleigh Salterton Pebbles and Otter Sandstones. A continuous climb to Crowcombe takes the line to a summit, about 400 ft. above sea level, between the Brendon and Quantock Hills.

A steady descent to Williton, through the valley of the Doniford Stream, is followed by a widening of the valley as it reaches the Bristol Channel and Watchet. From here the route returns inland over the Shales, Marls and Limestones of the Washford River valley. A summit of about 150 ft. above sea level is gained at Washford, from whence the line descends onto the coastal Alluvium at Blue Anchor. An almost level course, roughly parallel to the coast, is then followed to Minehead.

All maps are to the scale of 25" to 1 mile, unless otherwise stated.

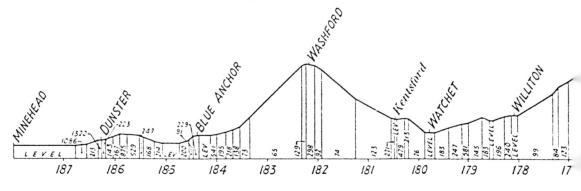

County Council who had purchased the property. A Light Railway Order had been obtained in November 1973 and services commenced between Minehead and Blue Anchor on 28th March 1976. Operation was extended to Williton on 28th August 1976, to Stogumber on 7th May 1978 and to Bishops Lydeard on 9th June 1979. Sadly for all concerned, a number of obstacles were raised to prevent operation to Taunton again, but hopefully visitors and the local community alike will benefit one day from a completely restored railway.

PASSENGER SERVICES

The initial service on the branch comprised four return journeys, weekdays only - regular Sunday trains were not provided until 1926. By 1869, there were six trains each way but in 1890, only four were provided, with an extra trip on Saturdays. In 1906, the basic service was seven trains, with an additional one on Mondays. At the beginning of World War I, there were eight return journeys, but as part of national economy measures, this was halved in 1917.

By 1921, services were back to six trains each way, with an extra one on Mondays and Saturdays. In 1926, there were seven trains, two of the down services carrying slip coaches from Paddington. On Sundays, there was one return working on the branch, with an additional trip between Minehead and Williton. With the increase in holiday traffic, the summer timetable for 1928 showed eleven weekday and two Sunday trains on the branch. Summer Sunday services were increased to five by 1934.

Wartime restrictions reduced the frequency to seven trains, weekdays only, in 1944. By 1950, the peak summer timetable showed eleven weekday and five Sunday journeys, with extras on Fridays and Sundays which included through trains to Paddington and to Wolverhampton. Ten years later, the service was similar, with fifteen trains running each way on Saturdays.

In the final decade, ten weekday services were normally provided, with five or six on summer Sundays. There were still some through trains; for example, on summer Saturdays in 1968, there were two to Paddington and two to Bristol.

Dieselisation did little to improve speed, the journey to Taunton taking about 55 minutes compared with 60 on most steam services.

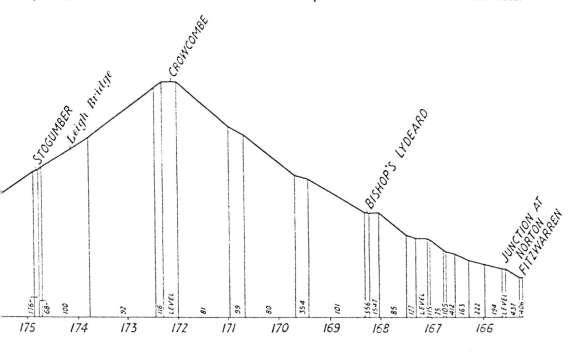

TAUNTON

1. This eastward view shows the arrangement that existed until the quadrupling of the tracks in 1931, when an island platform was added. On the right is the water tank of the locomotive depot, which was provided with a repair shop in 1932.   (Lens of Sutton)

The first station consisted of two platforms, end to end, on the south side of the line, both having roofs extending over the track.   This arrangement was altered when through running commenced and in 1868 the station was rebuilt to the plan shown on this first edition map of 1886.   In 1895, the station was further rebuilt and more bay platforms provided.   The Grand Western Canal had once allowed barges to pass from Bridgwater to Tiverton but in 1896 its disused aqueduct, shown south of the station, was replaced by a railway bridge.   This allowed avoiding lines to be laid, goods facilities to be extended and a new locomotive shed to be built.   The River Tone is lower right.

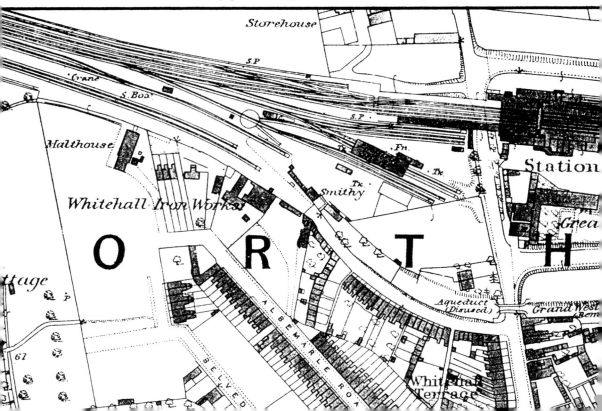

2. The Minehead branch train commonly used one of the bay platforms on the down side. The train is standing at the only one to be usable in 1990, although the canopy on the right had long gone. (Lens of Sutton)

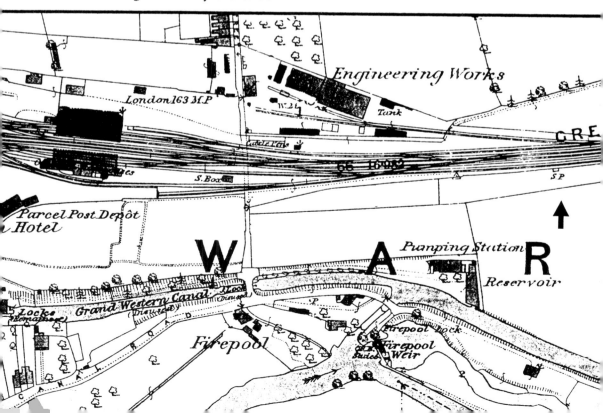

3. The 1931 improvements gave four through platforms of at least 1200 ft. in length. This is a westward view in 1955, the chimneys of the earlier station being visible in the background. (Lens of Sutton)

4. Unlike the up side, the buildings on the down sided remained untouched by the alterations of the early 1930s. Milk churns were still commonplace on passenger stations when this photograph was taken in July 1955. They are behind the beetle-shaped Standard Vanguard. (Lens of Sutton)

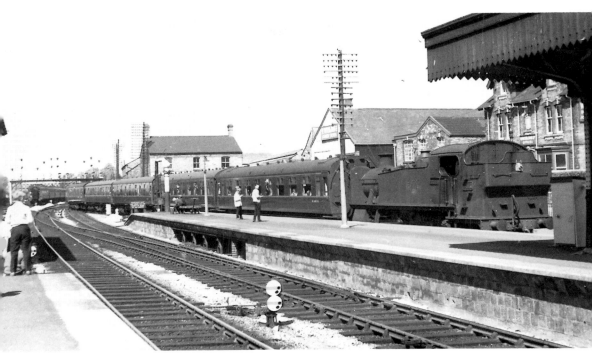

5. Viewed from platform 6, 2-6-2T no. 6113 runs into the bay platform with a train from Minehead in about 1961. West Station signal box is on the left, four boxes being necessary to work the station after 1931. (C.L.Caddy)

6. The Minehead to Manchester (Saturdays only) service stands at platform 7 on 8th September 1962. These through services for holidaymakers were still well patronised at that time, particularly by visitors to Butlin's Holiday Camp. (C.L.Caddy)

7. No. 6337, one of the extensive 4300 class, passes the squatting spotters in August 1963, with another through train from Minehead. With many of the trains from Barnstaple also terminating here, there was much railway activity to observe, particularly on summer Saturdays. (C.L.Caddy)

8. Two photographs from February 1969, illustrate the complexity of mechanical signalling at that time. The front seat passenger in a Minehead bound DMU could enjoy this panorama before leaving Taunton. (C.G.Maggs)

9. Beyond the footbridge, the line passes under the A358 before reaching Silk Mill crossing. On the down side, eight sidings were still in use for engineering purposes in 1990. The semaphore signals were displaced five years earlier. (C.G.Maggs)

NORTON FITZWARREN

10.   Although a junction for the Minehead
branch from 1862, a station was not opened
here until 1st August 1873.   Two platforms
sufficed until the 1931 quadrupling.
(Lens of Sutton)

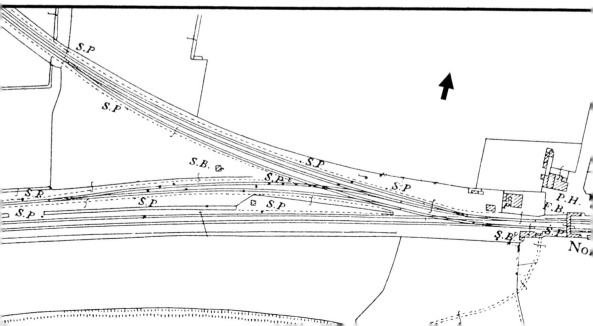

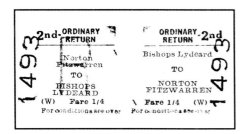

11. The Minehead lines curve to the right, the Barnstaple lines diverging to the left from them, in the distance. The roof of the Railway Hotel is on the right, beyond the small goods shed. (Lens of Sutton)

The 1929 edition has the double track from Taunton on the right, with those to Exeter on the left (lower). Above them are the single lines to Barnstaple and to Minehead, the line parallel to the latter being a long siding. Lower left are the banks of the Grand Western Canal.

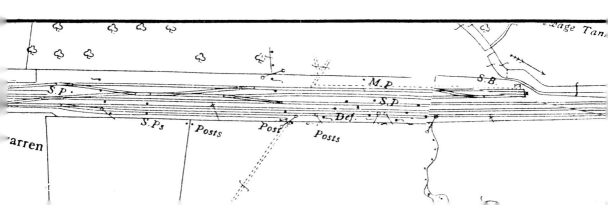

12. Following the quadrupling, two island platforms were built, linked by a footbridge from which this picture of a train from Barnstaple was taken. No. 3443 *Chaffinch* is running alongside the new station buildings, which were closed on 30th October 1961. Freight facilities were withdrawn on 6th July 1964 and the signal box was closed in March 1970. (Lens of Sutton)

14. In 1983, part of the up relief line, which was still connected to the Minehead branch, was reopened as the siding for the Taunton Cider Co. An HST races west on 7th April 1985, past the fenced off siding which still provides a connection to the branch for the transfer of stock. In the background is part of a former Government Depot which once had extensive sidings. (M. Turvey)

13. A westward view from the public footbridge, in July 1934, shows the extent of the goods yard, which had a 30cwt. capacity crane. The signal box is on the extreme left. (Mowat coll.)

BISHOPS LYDEARD

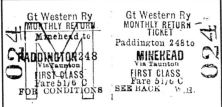

15. An up train waits for a train from Taunton to clear the single line from Norton Fitzwarren. The station master's house is opposite the signal box. (Lens of Sutton)

The 1904 map indicates the position of the 2-ton capacity goods crane.

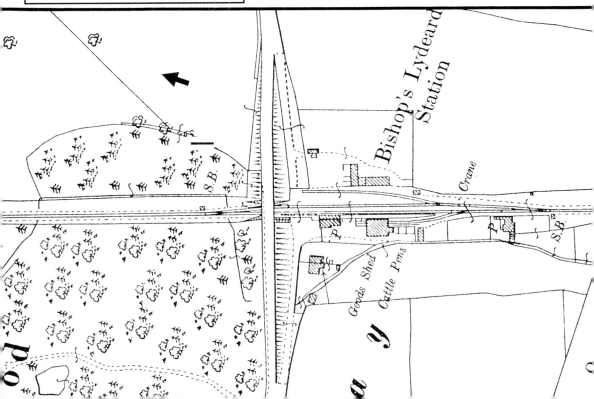

16. No. 6110 arrives from Norton Fitzwarren, the track from there having been doubled on 7th June 1936. The goods siding on the left was added around 1900 and a further siding to a Government food store (extreme left) followed during World War II. This siding was closed on 12th August 1966, general freight facilities having been withdrawn on 6th July 1964 (C.L.Caddy)

18. In the final years of the branch, through trains were diesel hauled, this example being no. D6336. Taunton locomotive depot had closed in October 1964 and steam had vanished from the Western Region within two years. (C.L.Caddy)

17. The signal box was opened in 1906 and closed on 1st March 1970, when the station became unstaffed. BR class 3 2-6-2T approaches the crossover in 1962. (C.L.Caddy)

WEST SOMERSET.—Great Western.					[b 1&2 class.			
Down.	gov	mrn	aft	aft	gov			
Bristol 12.dep	6 15	9 2	12 10	2/26	5 41			
Taunton......dep	8 0	11 25	1 55	4c10	7 0			
Norton Fitzwarren	8 5	11 31	2 2	4c15	7 6			
Bishop's Lydeard	8 15	11 39	2 10	4c25	7 15			
Crowcombe Heath	8 27	11 50	2 21	4c36	7 25			
Stogumber ..[field	8 34	11 56	2 27	4c42	7 31			
Williton.........	8 43	12 4	2 35	4c51	7 41			
Watchet 11......	8 49	12 10	2 41	4c56	7 47			
Washford	8 56	12 17	2 48	5 c 37	7 54			
Blue Anchor	9 3	12 23	2 54	5c10	8 0			
Dunster.........	9 10	12 30	3 1	5c16	8 7			
Minehead *....arr	9 15	12 35	3 5	5c2	8 13			
Up.	gov	mrn	aft	gov	aft			
Minehead ....dep	8 10	11 30	1 0	5 50	7c10			
Dunster..........	8 15	11 35	1 4	5 55	7c15			
Blue Anchor	8 21	11 41	1 10	6 1	7c21			
Washford	8 29	11 49	1 18	6 9	7c29			
Watchet 11	8 36	11 56	1 24	6 17	7c36			
Williton	8 44	12 5	1 31	6 25	7c44			
Stogumber ..[field	8 54	12 13	1 39	6 34	7c53			
Crowcombe Heath	9 4	12 21	1 47	6 43	8 c 1			
Bishop's Lydeard	9 13	12 30	1 56	6 50	8 c 9			
Nortn Fitzwrrn	12 9	24	12 40	2 5	6 58	8c17		
Taunton 13,12 arr	9 29	12 45	2 10	7 3	8c2			
Bristol 13. arr	11 50	2 50	3 37	9 45	12 8			

c Saturdays only. • Station for Porlock, Lynmouth, Lynton, Ilfracombe, &c.

February 1890

19. A loop was shown on the 1886 survey but there was no platform or signal box. These were added in 1906, when the loop was extended at the south end to 1000 ft. and signalled for use by passenger trains. This northward view shows the loop five years before it was taken out of use on 1st March 1970. (C.L.Caddy)

20. This photograph was taken on 9th June 1979 - the day passenger services from Minehead were resumed. Sadly the Park Royal DMU could not reach Taunton, even if it had been spelled correctly.
(Dorset Transport Circle)

21. No. 7820 *Dinmore Manor* was in use on
BR from 1950 to 1965. After 14 years in the
Barry breaker's yard it went to the Gwili Railway, and is seen at Bishops Lydeard, shortly
after arrival in 1985. (M. Turvey)

TAUNTON, WATCHET, and MINEHEAD.—Great Western.

Down.				Week Days.						Up.				Week Days.					
			b	mrn	mrn	mrn	aft	aft	aft	aft	Miles			mrn	b	mrn	aft	aft	aft
Taunton ....dep.	7	20	8	0	1040	1150	4	4	33	6	20	7	45	Minehead.........dep.	8	5	9	35	1050
Norton Fitzwarren....	7	16	8	8	1048	1158	51	....	6	25	7	53	11	Dunster	8	12	9	40	1056
Bishop's Lydeard	7	31	8	15	1056	12	6	2	2	....	6	34	8	0	31	Blue Anchor	8	17
Crowcombe	7	43	8	25	11	7	1216	2	12	....	6	44	8	13	51	Washford.............	8	23
Stogumber	7	49	8	31	1115	1223	18	....	6	50	8	15	8	Watchet	8	29	9	55	1114
Williton	7	56	8	39	1123	1229	2	23	....	6	57	8	26	91	Williton	8	37	10	0	1121
Watchet	8	2	8	45	1129	1235	2	31	....	7	3	8	32	13	Stogumber	8	45	....	1129
Washford.............	8	10	8	53	1137	1243	2	47	....	7	15	8	44	154	Crowcombe	8	53	....	1140
Blue Anchor	8	18	8	58	1142	1248	2	47	....	7	19	8	47	194	Bishop's Lydeard ...	9	1	....	1148
Dunster	8	22	9	2	1146	1252	2	47	....	7	19	8	47	22	Norton Fitzwarren	2	9	7	....	1154
Minehead ...... arr.	8	29	9	10	1153	1	0	2	55	3	20	7	25	8	55	24	Taunton 22, 26..arr.	9	15	1050	12

b Mondays only.   * Station for Porlock, Lynmouth, Lynton, &c.

July 1906

22. The two Park Royal DMUs await departure for Minehead on 6th September 1987, while the stock of the "Quantock Belle" stands in the distance. More recently, it has resided in a new siding in the car park.
(P.G.Barnes)

23. DMUs are regularly used between Bishops Lydeard and Williton, where passengers are able to transfer to a steam hauled train. The goods shed track was relaid in 1976 and the building has since been used for carriage restoration. (R.E.Ruffell)

24. The station is the headquarters of the West Somerset Railway Association and facilities include a bookshop and model railway display. An old style red telephone box has recently been added to enhance the historic aura of the environs. (V.Mitchell)

25. Fortunately the box was not demolished after the lever frame was removed by BR. When photographed in 1989, all points were still worked from ground frames. (R.E.Ruffell)

CROWCOMBE

26. An early postcard view shows bridge rail on longitudinal timbers still to be in use, this design dating from broad gauge days. The 1st edition of the Ordnance Survey showed a passing loop but no down platform. (Lens of Sutton)

The 1904 revision shows the original name. "Heathfield" was officially dropped in November 1889 to avoid confusion with stations of that name in South Devon and East Sussex.

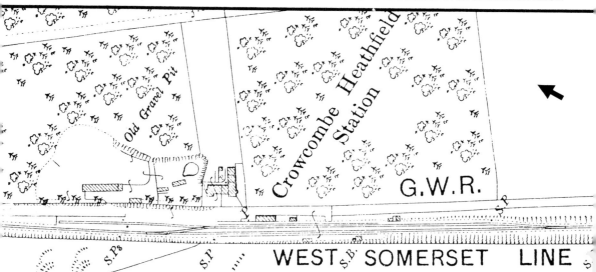

27. Fourteen members of the 4500 class have been saved but not no. 5525. Beyond the 40mph sign is the tablet catcher, both installed during the line improvements of 1934 and seen in about 1958. The road on the bridge in the background is 403 ft above sea level. (C.L.Caddy)

28. The signal box was built in 1879 and closed on 27th March 1966. It was burnt down on 5th March 1967, when the station became unstaffed. In 1990 work was in progress to replace the box with one from Ebbw Vale Tinplate Works, using the frame from Frome North. This and the next picture date from October 1965. (C.L.Caddy)

29. The siding in the foreground once carried stone from W.J.King's Triscombe Quarry, two miles to the east. This produced fine grained sandstone and quartzite, of use in building work and road making. The waiting room on the down platform was demolished in 1967, goods facilities having been withdrawn on 6th July 1964. (C.L.Caddy)

30. Doors of the Gloucester DMU are open as the train was ahead of time on 20th June 1989. The delightfully situated station won an ARPS Best Station Award in 1985 and will eventually have its loop fully restored. (R.E.Ruffell)

LEIGH BRIDGE CROSSING

31.   To increase the line capacity this additional passing place was opened on 16th July 1934, the box being open from 9.35am until 7.35pm, in the summer only. Closure date was 5th May 1964. The nearby level crossing was fitted with automatic lights in 1978. (Mowat coll.)

STOGUMBER

32. The station site being on the side of a deep valley, the stone building had to be remote from the lightweight wooden platform. The cattle dock in the distance was unusual in having a flight of steps to it. Note the even steeper steps for the lampman. (C.L.Caddy)

The 1886 survey shows that the bridge over the lane was built to accommodate two tracks although the extra siding was not added until later.

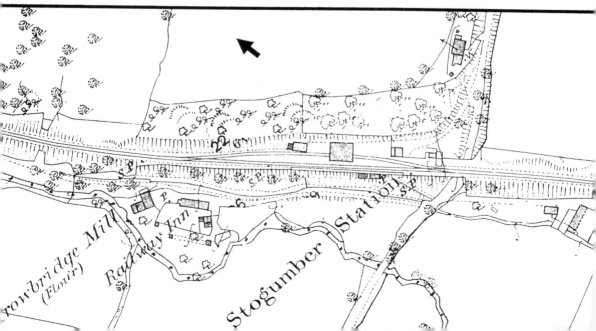

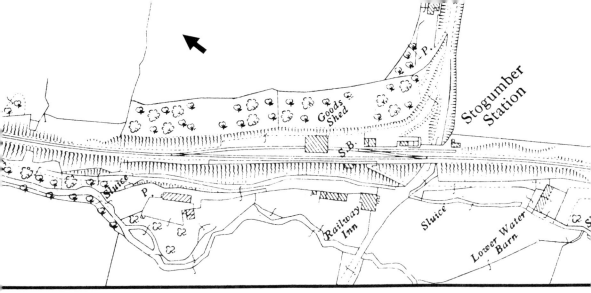

The 1904 edition reveals that the platform had been lengthened and that a new Railway Inn had been built. The signal box (S.B.) was replaced by two ground frames in April 1926.

33. Another 1965 view shows the dangerous foot crossing, visibility being restricted by the goods shed. Staff had been withdrawn ten years earlier but the goods shed remained in use until 19th August 1963. It contained a 2-ton crane and was demolished in 1965. (C.L.Caddy)

Great Western Railway
GOVERNMENT RATE TICKET
Soldier, Sailor, Police, &c., on Duty.
STOGUMBER TO
WILLITON
PARLIAMENTARY [THIRD CLASS]
Issued subject to the conditions stated
on the Cos. Time Bills (E.S)
Williton   Williton
035

34.   The 16.45 from Taunton arrives on 30th June 1967, by which time mini-skirts were in vogue but goods sidings were not.   The concrete sleepers suggest that track relaying is imminent.   (C.G.Maggs)

35.   Seen on the last day of BR services, the concrete sleepered track was devoid of a proper foot crossing to the platform.   In 1990, the southern timber part of the platform was missing, leaving the shelter isolated and unusable.   Passengers used the stone-faced section at the far end, which has recently been extended northwards in timber. (E.Wilmshurst)

36. Castle Hill makes an attractive backdrop as a Minehead bound DMU leaves the curving track of the narrow valley and approaches the south points of Williton loop in June 1966. (T.Wright)

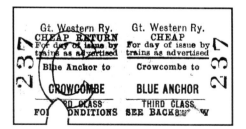

LONDON, TAUNTON, WATCHET, and MINEHEAD.—Great Western.																					

Down. Week Days only.

Miles		ngt	mrn	mrn	mrn	aft	aft	aft	aft	
	Paddington Station,									
10	London ....dep.	12 0	5 30	7 30	10 45	1 30	...	3 30	4 15	....
—	Taunton ....dep.	8	2 10	37	12 17	1 48	4 46	5 45	6 20	7 46	....
2	Norton Fitzwarren ..	5	8 10	44	12 24	1 54	b	5 53	b	7 53	....
5	Bishop's Lydeard	8	15	10	52	12 32	2 3	b	6 0	b	8 0	....
9	Crowcombe	8	25	11	3	12 42	2 13	b	6 11	b	8 12	....
11½	Stogumber	8	31	11	9	12 48	2 19	b	6 17	b	8 19	....
15	Williton	8	39	11	20	12 56	2 26	b	6 25	b	8 26	....
16½	Watchet	8	45	11	27	1	3	2 32	b	6 32	b	8 32	....
19	Washford	8	53	11	35	1	11	2 39	b	6 39	b	8 39	....
21¾	Blue Anchor	8	58	11	41	1	20	2 45	b	6 44	b	8 44	....
23	Dunster	9	6	11	50	1	28	2 53	b	6 51	b	8 51	....
24½	Minehead ¶ .... arr.	9	10	11	55	1	33	2 57	5	35	6 55	7	20	8 55	....

Up. Week Days only.

Miles		mrn	mrn	mrn	aft	aft	aft	aft	aft	
1½	Minehead ....dep.	8	7	9	26	10 45	1	5	2	36	4	13	7	5	9	20	....
3½	Dunster	8	12	9	31	10 52	1	11	2	36	4	16	7	10	9	25	....
3½	Blue Anchor	8	17	9	36	10 57	1	18	2	44	4	21	7	17	9	30	....
5½	Washford	8	23	9	42	11	41	25	2	50	4	28	7	23	9	36	....
8	Watchet	8	30	9	49	11	12	1	22	2	56	4	35	7	31	9	43	....
9¼	Williton	8	37	9	55	11	19	1	38	3	2	4	41	7	37	9	49	....
13	Stogumber	8	45	10	3	11	27	1	46	...	4	49	7	45	9	57	....
15¼	Crowcombe	8	53	10	11	11	40	1	54	3	16	4	59	7	54	10	5	....
19¼	Bishop's Lydeard ..	9	1	10	23	11	48	2	4	3	26	5	7	8	5	10	13	....
22	Norton Fitzwarren	20	9	10	....	11	57	2	19	....	5	16	8	15	10	24	....
24½	Taunton	15, 20 . arr.	9	15	10	35	12	22	2	43	3	55	21	8	20	10	30	....
	15	London (Pad.) arr.	....	1	30	4	20	5½	42	6	45	8	40	...	3	30	....

NOTES.

‡ Station for Porlock, Lynmouth, Lynton, &c.

☞ **For other Trains**

BETWEEN PAGE

Taunton and Norton Fitzwarren 20

a By slip carriage. *b* Leaves at 9 50 on Sunday nights. **b** Stops to set down from Bristol and beyond, Exeter and beyond, and Barnstaple and Ilfracombe Branch on informing the Guard at Taunton. *d* Leaves at 10 30 mrn. by slip carriage until 17th inst. *f* Arrives at 7 5 aft. until 18th inst. *k* Commences on 17th inst. ¶ For Coach Service between Minehead, Lynmouth, and Lynton, see page 1039.

July 1914

WILLITON

37. The station is close to the confluence of the north flowing Doniford Stream and another stream from the west, which normally passes *under* the railway in the foreground. Hence the flooding in 1877 and the opportunity to record a broad gauge train on the branch. (Lens of Sutton)

The first edition map of 1886 shows an arrangement which changed little in the ensuing 100 years, although it does mark two "hydrants". The bridge over the railway was built in 1873 and a 6-ton goods crane was provided later.

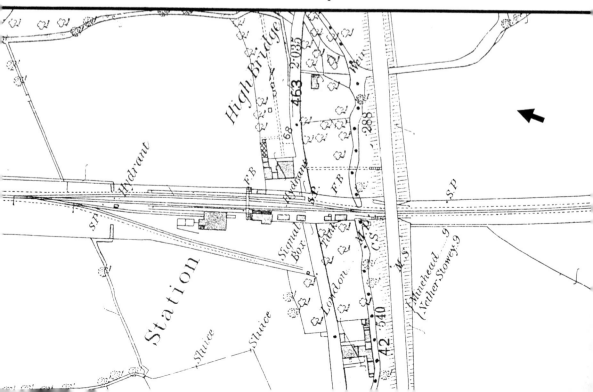

38. The wide gap between the tracks left when the broad gauge was converted to standard allowed the erection of a footbridge support and water columns, not present in the previous picture. The loop, signal box and footbridge all date from 1871. (Lens of Sutton)

39. The loop was lengthened in 1906 and again in 1934, necessitating the widening of the bridge over the stream in the foreground. On the left is the post carrying a lamp to illuminate the conventional tablet catcher, the automatic catcher being close to the level crossing. (Lens of Sutton)

40. An October 1965 picture includes the weed covered goods yard, which closed on 6th July 1964. The wooden footbridge was replaced by this steel lattice one in the 1920s. The population of Williton rose from 1400 in 1901 to 1900 in 1951. (C.L.Caddy)

41. Williton and Blue Anchor were the only passing places on the route in the final years of public ownership. The points were designed for trains to pass at 40mph. The scene was recorded in June 1966. (T.Wright)

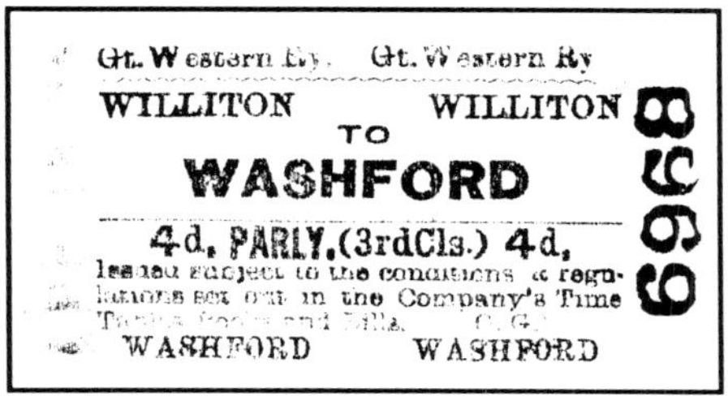

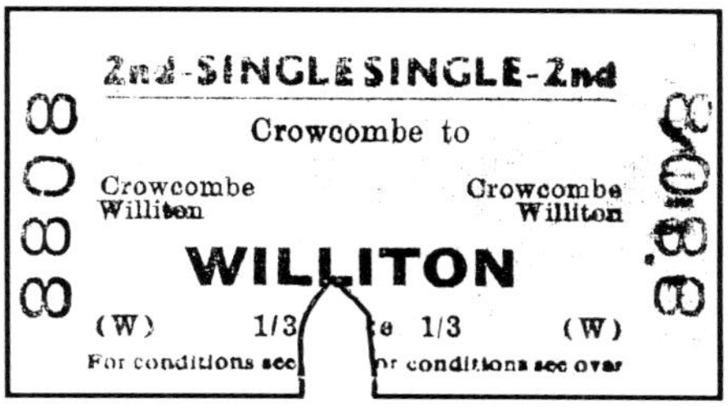

42. By the time that this photograph was taken on 14th March 1970, the long radius point had been removed and the bridge over the stream cut back to single track. The large water tank had also been removed. (E.Wilmshurst)

LONDON, TAUNTON, WATCHET, and MINEHEAD.

Down.	Week Days.												Suns.	
	ngt.	mrn	mrn	mrn	mrn	aft	aft	aft	aft	aft	aft	aft	mrn	aft
12 London (Pad.) ....dep.	12b0	....	5 30	9 0	9 15	12 5	1 30	....	3K30	3K30	4 30	T	9 10	2 30
Taunton ....dep.	7 25	8 10	10 50	12 15	2 0	3 15	4 40	5 16	6 7	6 30	8 15	....	2 15	7 40
Norton Fitzwarren.......	7 25	8 15	10 55	....	2 6	....	....	5 21	....	6 35	8 22	....	2 21	7 46
Bishop's Lydeard	7 35	8 27	11 5	12 27	2 20	....	4 52	5 30	....	6 44	8 31	....	2 30	7 55
Crowcombe..............	7 46	8 37	11 16	Cc	2 30	....	5 3	5 40	....	6 55	8 41	....	2 41	8 6
Stogumber	....	8 43	11 22	Cc	2 36	....	....	5 46	....	7 1	8 47	....	2 46	8 12
Williton	8 2	8 49	11 32	12 46	2 43	3 43	5 15	5 54	....	7 9	8 53	11 25	2 54	8 20
Watchet...	8 12	8 55	11 38	12 51	2 50	3 50	5 21	6 0	....	7 15	8 58	11 30	3 0	8 26
Washford (for Cleeve	8 18	9 1	11 44	12 57	2 56	....	5 27	6 6	....	7 21	9 4	....	3 6	8 32
Blue Anchor..... [Abbey)	8 26	9 8	11 49	Cc	3 1	....	5 32	6 16	Cc	7 29	9 12	....	3 11	8 37
Dunster	8 33	9 15	11 56	1 7	3 8	Nn	5 38	6 23	Cc	7 36	9 19	....	3 19	8 45
Minehead B.........arr.	8 37	9 19	12 0	1 11	3 12	4 4	5 42	6 27	6 52	7 40	9 23	11 45	3 23	8 49
Lynton & Lynmouth "	....	11 30	....	....	....	6 15	....	....	....	....	....	....	....	....

Up.	Week Days.												Suns.	
	mrn	mrn	mrn	mrn	aft	aft	aft	aft	aft	aft	aft	aft	aft	aft
Lynton & Lynm'th dep	....	....	....	8 20	....	....	....	....	2 45	....	....	T	....	....
Minehead.......... "	7 30	8 55	9 35	11 0	1 35	2 10	4 15	6 5	7 15	9 0	10 0	10 45	5 30	9 15
Dunster	7 35	9 0	....	11 5	....	2 15	4 20	6 10	7 20	9 5	10 5	10 50	5 35	9 20
Blue Anchor	7 40	9 7	9h40	11 10	....	2 20	4 25	6 15	7 27	9 11	10 10	10 55	5 40	9 25
Washford (for Cleeve	7 47	9 14	....	11 17	1 47	2 28	4 32	6 22	7 34	9 18	10 17	11 2	5 48	9 33
Watchet ....(Abbey)	7 53	9 20	9 51	11 24	1 53	2 35	4 38	6 28	7 39	9 24	10 23	11 10	5 55	9 41
Williton	8 1	9 24	9 56	11 31	1 58	2 44	4 44	6 37	7 43	9 29	10 28	11 14	6 2	9 48
Stogumber	8 9	9 32	....	11 39	....	2 52	4 52	6 45	....	9 37	....	....	6 10	9 57
Crowcombe..............	8 18	9 40	....	11 48	....	3 0	5 5	6 56	....	9 45	10 44	....	6 18	10 6
Bishop's Lydeard	8 28	9 48	....	11 56	2 18	3 7	5 12	7 5	....	9 52	10 52	....	6 26	10 14
Norton Fitzwarren 22..	8 34	....	....	12 3	....	3 14	....	7 14	8 10	9 59	....	....	6 32	10 21
Taunton 7, 17, 22 arr.	8 39	9 57	10 30	12 8	2 28	3 19	5 22	7 19	8 15	10 4	11 2	....	6 37	10 26
17 London (Pad.)..arr.	11 45	....	1 15	4 5	5 30	6 50	9 0	....	11 20	....	7 10	....	9 30	3 5

B Station for Porlock, and Lynton and Lynmouth, by Motor Coach. b Departs Paddington at 9 50 aft. on Sundays.
Cc Stops to set down from London on notice being given to the guard at Taunton.
h Calls to take up for Bristol and beyond on notice being given to the Station Master at Blue Anchor before 9 30 mrn. K Slip Carriage.
Nn Stops to set down from Taunton and beyond on notice being given to the guard at Taunton. T Wednesdays, Fridays, and Saturdays.
. For OTHER TRAINS between Taunton and Norton Fitzwarren, see page 22 and above.

August 1928

43. A northward view on 8th October 1979 shows that both platforms had been signalled for the starting of trains to Minehead since reopening under private management. Note the absence of water columns at that time. (S.C.Nash)

44. The fireman uncouples 1934-built no. 6412 on 7th April 1985, as passengers wander over the foot crossing to continue their journey to Bishops Lydeard in the two-car Craven DMU. The locomotive had earlier spent ten years on the Dart Valley Railway. (M.Turvey)

45. Smoke rises from the Maybach diesel engine as no. D7017 is revved up in the up platform on 6th June 1987. The Hymek class 35 is used only occasionally as it is too heavy for regular use on the line. (P.G.Barnes)

46. September 1987 was notable for the return to service of ex-S&DJR 2-8-0 no.53808, after having been out of steam for 23 years. Note the four point rods and numerous wires that are required to work the north end of the station. (P.G.Barnes)

47. After closure of the yard, the former goods shed siding was reconnected in January 1967 for use by the engineers. In 1983 the other sidings were relaid and Williton has become a centre of activity for the Diesel & Electric Group. D7017 is on the left and class 14 no. D9551 is in the centre. The van on the right stands on a siding which will lead to a proposed new locomotive shed, an ex-Swindon machinery store. (V.Mitchell)

48. Another photograph from April 1990 shows the booking hall entrance and parts of the footbridge from Trowbridge awaiting erection between the platforms, where the 1871 structure stood. (V.Mitchell)

2nd - FORCES/MM LEAVE	FORCES/MM - 2nd LEAVE
Watchet to	
Watchet Minehead	Watchet Minehead
MINEHEAD	
(W)	(W)
I/II Fare I/II	
For conditions see over	For conditions see over

4971

4971

DONIFORD BRIDGE HALT

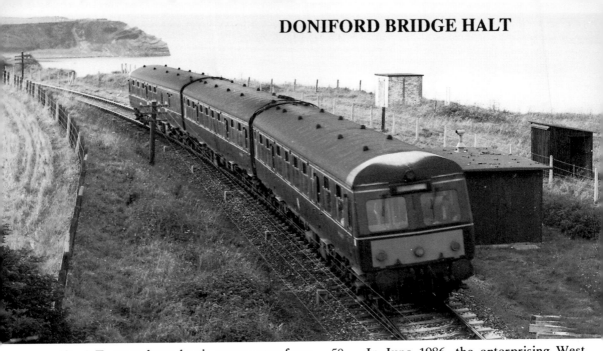

49. A Taunton-bound train curves away from the coast in September 1965, leaving behind the spectacular exposures of the complex geology of the area. The concrete monuments at the ballast shoulder helped staff to return the track to its correct position after speeding trains moved it towards the sea. (T.Wright)

50. In June 1986, the enterprising West Somerset Railway opened Doniford Beach Halt for the benefit of holidaymakers. The platform components came from Montacute, on the Taunton-Yeovil line, and the pagoda parts from Cove, on the Exe Valley route. Assembly was well advanced when photographed on 16th April 1990. (V.Mitchell)

51. This westward view was taken between 31st March 1862 and 16th July 1874, when Watchet was the terminus of the branch. In the foreground are the harbour lines, opened in June 1862, and on the left is the locomotive depot. (Somerset County Library)

52. The Eastern Pier is seen in about 1936, with a crowd of people looking down at the seaplane on the deck of the SDJR's steamship *Radstock*. Much of the shunting at the harbour was undertaken by a horse. (C.G.Maggs coll.)

The 1886 map has the line from Taunton lower right and the terminus of the West Somerset Mineral Railway top centre. The terminal building is now in commercial use.

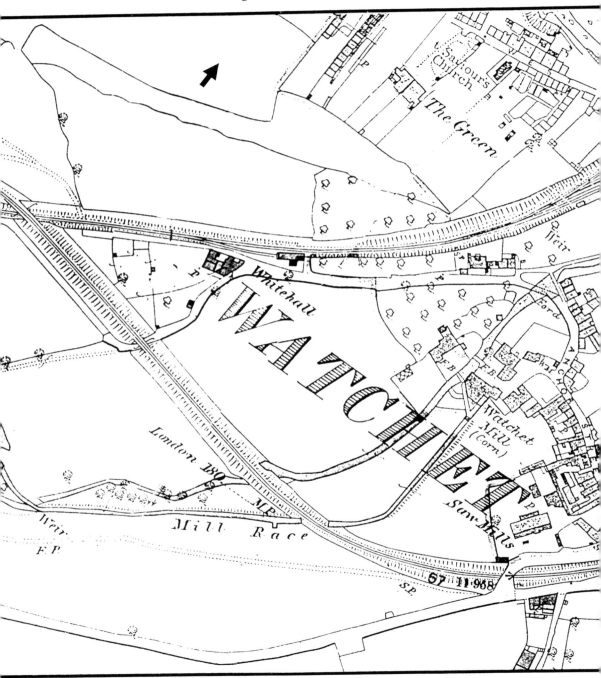

53. The goods shed is largely obscured as the 4500 class 2-6-2T arrives from Minehead in about 1958. Beyond the railings, a wagon stands on the harbour headshunt which was at a lower level than the running line. (C.L.Caddy)

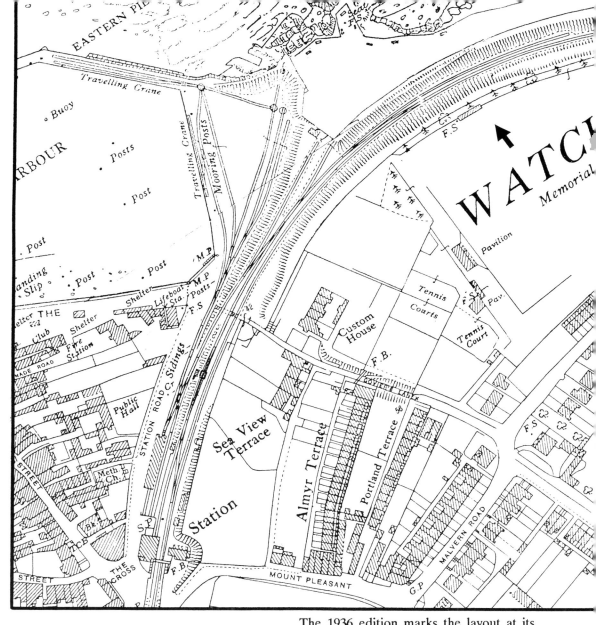

The 1936 edition marks the layout at its optimum, with a long siding running parallel to the Taunton line, upper right. The number of inhabitants grew from 1880 in 1901 to 2600 fifty years later.

54. No. D6336 heads west as a Western National Bristol KSW turns by the goods shed. General freight facilities were withdrawn on 19th May 1965, this photograph dating from that era. (C.L.Caddy)

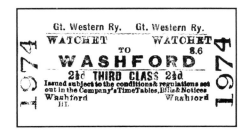

55. An October 1965 view includes the then new BR logo and an SW board, which ordered the driver to sound his whistle in advance of the footpath crossing. The building is at right angles to the track, as it was built to serve as a terminus. (C.L.Caddy)

57. The harbour lines were closed on 19th May 1965 and after they were lifted only the weighbridge remained, in front of the weighhouse. The headshunt could only accommodate a locomotive and eight wagons, severely restricting traffic through the port. (T.Wright)

LONDON, TAUNTON, WATCHET, and MINEHEAD.—Great Western.

Miles	Down.	Week Days.								Suns.		Miles	Up.	Week Days.						Suns.	
		ngt.	mrn	S	mrn	mrn	aft	aft		aft	aft	mrn aft			mrn	mrn	mrn		aft	aft	aft	aft		aft	aft
	12 London (Pad.)....dep.	12 50	5 30	9 0	10 30	1 15	1 30	3 30	5		3 30	4 30	9 10		Lynton & Lynm'th dep		9 0				2 45				...
—	Taunton ....dep.	8 15	10 25	12 10	1 45	3 10	4 39	6 5		6 35	8 15	2 15		Minehead.......... "	7 30 9	21	1110		1 20	4 40	6 45	9 0	10 15		3 45	9 15
2	Norton Fitzwarren	8 21	10 31	12 21	1 51	...	4 35	...		6 41	8 21	2 21	1½	Dunster	7 35 9		7 11		1 25	4 46	6 51	9	10 20		3 50	9 20
5	Bishop's Lydeard	8 32	10 40	12 31	2 1	...	4 45	...		6 50	8 30	2 30	3½	Blue Anchor......	7 40 9	14	7 17		1 30	4 51	6 56	9 11	10 25		3 55	9 25
9	Crowcombe	8 43	10 51	12 43	2 14	...	4 57	...		7 2	8 41	2 41	5½	Washford (for Cleeve	7 48 9	22	11 32		1 39	4 59	7 5	9 19	10 32		4 3	9 33
11½	Stogumber	8 49	10 57	12 49	2 20	...	5 3	...		7 8	8 47	...	8	Watchet ......[Abbey]	7 54 9	28	11 46		1 46	5 7	7 12	9 26	10 40		4 11	9 41
15	Williton	8 57	11 4	12 58	2 28	...	3 44	5 13		7 18	8 55	2 53	8 20	9½	Williton	8 1	9 35	11 46		1 52	5 12	7 19	9 33	10 43		4 15	9 48
16¾	Watchet	9 3	11 10	1 5	2 34	3 54	5 19	...		7 24	9 6	3 08	26	13	Stogumber	8 10	9 44	11 55		2 15	2 17	28	9 42	...		...	10 4
19	Washford (for Cleeve	9 9	11 16	1 12	2 40	...	5 25	...		7 31	9 6	3 3	6 8 32	15½	Crowcombe.........	8 19	9 53	12 5		2 13	5 30	7 38	9 51	11 4		...	10 12
21¼	Blue Anchor...... [Abbey]	9 15	11 24	1 30	2 45	...	5 31 Aa	...		7 36	9 13	3 11	8 37	19¾	Bishop's Lydeard	8 28	10 1	12 13		2 21	5 39	7 47	9 59	11 12		...	10 19
23	Dunster	9 22	11 31	1 38	2 52	Nn	5 38	...		7 43	9 20	3 19	8 45	22¼	Norton Fitzwarren 22..	8 37	10 8	12 21		2 28	5 46	7 55	10 7	...		...	10 23
24½	Minehead ⓑ .... arr.	9 26	11 35	1 42	2 56	4 10	5 42	7 5		7 47	9 24	3 23	8 49	24½	Taunton 7, 17, 22 arr.	8 42	10 13	12 25		2 33	5 51	8 0	10 13	11 28		...	10 24
	Lynton & Lynmouth "	11 30	...	...	5 0	...	...			...	...	...		167¼	17 London (Pad.) ... arr.		1 15	4 5		6 50	9 0	10 7	10 7 10	...		3 5

Aa Stops to set down from London on notice being given to the Guard at Taunton. **B** Station for Porlock, and Lynton and Lynmouth, by Motor Coach.
b Departs Paddington at 9 50 aft. on Sundays. **K** Slip Carriage. **Nn** Stops to set down from Taunton and beyond on notice being given to the Guard at Taunton.
S Saturdays only.

August 1926

56. Another 1965 picture includes the base of the signal box (left), which closed on 11th August 1926, being replaced by ground frames. On the right is a covered loading area. (C.L.Caddy)

58. As in the case of most branch lines, local bus operators were serious competitors for the railway although the bus still takes 48 minutes for the 17 miles to Taunton. Bristol LWL5G no. 1612 is seen in June 1966 by the station footbridge, which was the only one on the line for many years. (T.Wright)

60. A shopper waits to join the Park Royal set on 11th September 1987, a small amount of local traffic being carried on the restored railway. The goods shed was occupied by Watchet Marine Ltd in 1990. (P.G.Barnes)

59. A Taunton bound DMU approaches the dangerous footpath crossing in June 1966, the path earlier passing over three more tracks. Prior to the reopening of the line, treadle operated lights were fitted here to warn pedestrians of approaching trains. (T.Wright)

Paper mills were established west of Watchet in about 1835, power being supplied by the Washford River. Messrs. Wansbrough, Peach & Date became the Wansbrough Paper Co. by 1900, products ranging from envelopes to wallpaper. The private siding, shown on this 1936 map, was connected to the main line

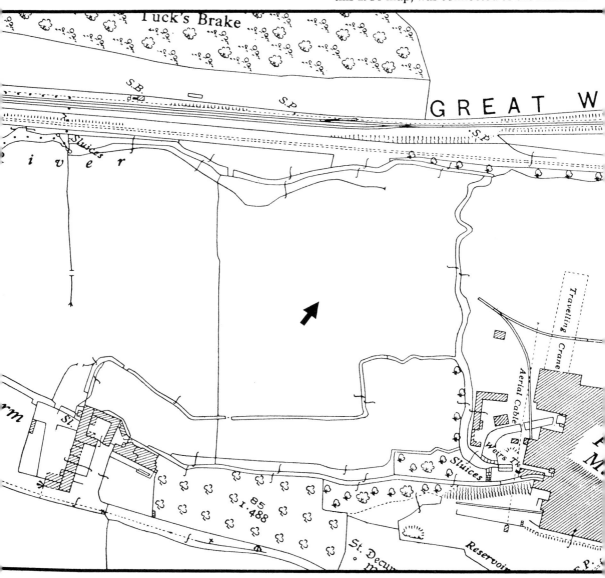

from 31st January 1929 until 2nd February 1965. Across the map is the trackbed of the West Somerset Mineral Railway (now a public footpath) and upper left is the double track of Kentsford Loop used in summers between 10th July 1933 and 7th May 1964.

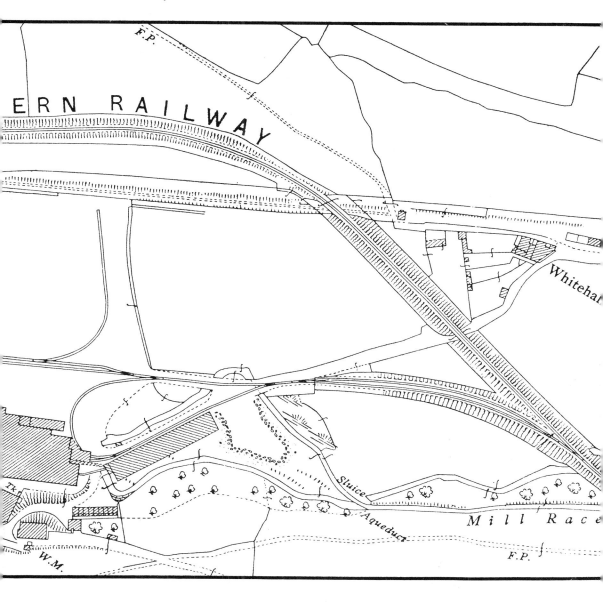

WEST SOMERSET
MINERAL RAILWAY

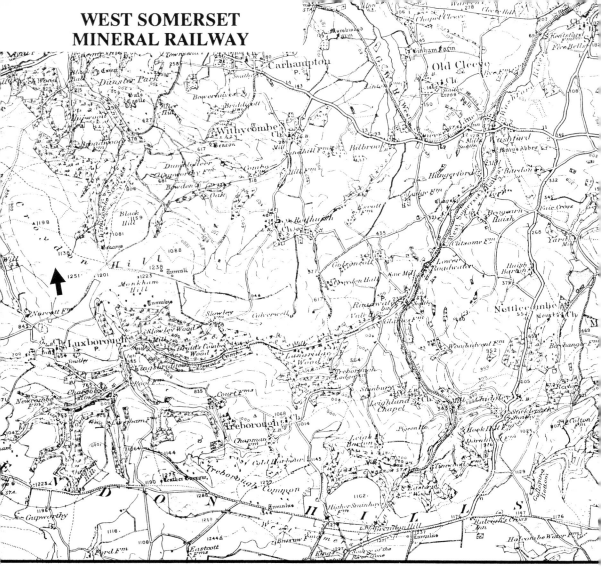

The 1" to 1 mile Ordnance Survey of 1896 marks the extent of the West Somerset Mineral Railway. Built under an Act of 1855, the standard gauge railway was intended primarily for carriage of iron ore from the mines in the Brendon Hills to Watchet, from where it would be sent by sea to South Wales. It was opened south to Roadwater in April 1857 and to Comberow in December of that year. A 1 in 4 rope worked incline had to be constructed from there, to gain height to the mining area. This was finished in March 1861, by which time improvements to Watchet Harbour were nearly complete.

The Minehead branch crossed over the line on a skew bridge (still in use today) and is shown running parallel for nearly two miles to Washford. There was no permanent connection between the two railways. The extension to Gupworthy was opened in September 1864 and passenger services commenced on 4th September 1865, between there and Watchet, passengers using the incline at their own risk.

A decline in the iron industry in 1883 was followed by a complete closure of the railway on 7th November 1898. The line was partially reopened, for mineral traffic only, from 1907 until 1910, and lifted during WWI.

The symbol for a mineral railway is used for the southern part of the line, although the unofficial carriage of passengers is recognised by marking a station near Gupworthy. The railway is well illustrated in *The Old Mineral Line* (Exmoor Press), available from Minehead station.

WASHFORD

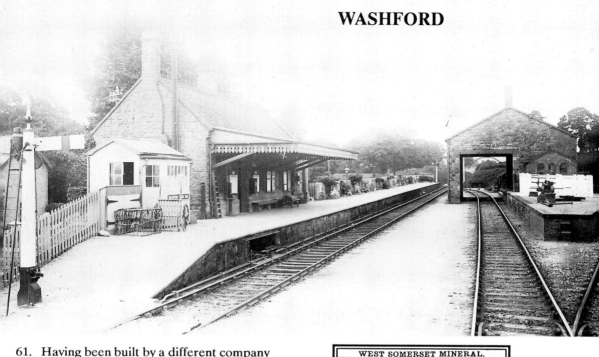

61. Having been built by a different company at a later date, the stations west of Watchet were dissimilar to those to the east. Well kept gardens and a cage for transport of small animals were traditional but the vending machine on the platform and the oil engine on the cattle dock heralded the change to mechanisation. (SDRT coll.)

The 1904 revision shows no changes to have taken place since the first survey.

WEST SOMERSET MINERAL.					
Up.		mrn	aft	**Down.**	mrn	aft
Watchet ..dep	9 15	3 0	Comberow..dep	11 0	4 15
Washford	9 25	3 10	Roadwater	1110	4 25
Roadwater	9 35	3 20	Washford	1120	4 35
Comberow..arr	9 45	3 30	Watchet 17..arr	1130	4 45

February 1890

WATCHET to the BRENDON HILLS.								
West Somerset Mineral.								
Down.	**Week**	**days.**			**Up.**	**Week Days.**		
From Bristol,	1,2,3	1,2,3	1&2	1&2		1,2,3	1&2	1,2,3	1&2
Taunton, &c.,	clss	clss	clss	clss		clss	clss	clss	clss
	mrn	mrn	aft	aft		mrn	mrn	aft	aft
Watchet ..dep	7 30	1043	3 0	6 25	Combe Row dp	8 30	1130	5 20	7 0
Washford	7 40	1053	3 40	6 34	Roadwater	8 45	1140	5 35	7 12
Roadwater ...	7 52	1043	3 5	6 44	Washford	9 0	1155	5 50	7 22
Combe Row ar	8 10	11 0	4 10	5 55	Watchet 10 ar	9 10	12 0	6 0	7 38

June 1869

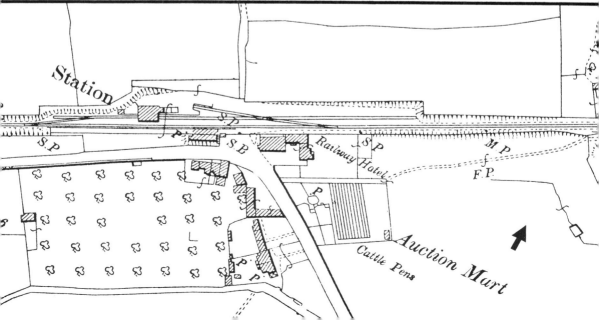

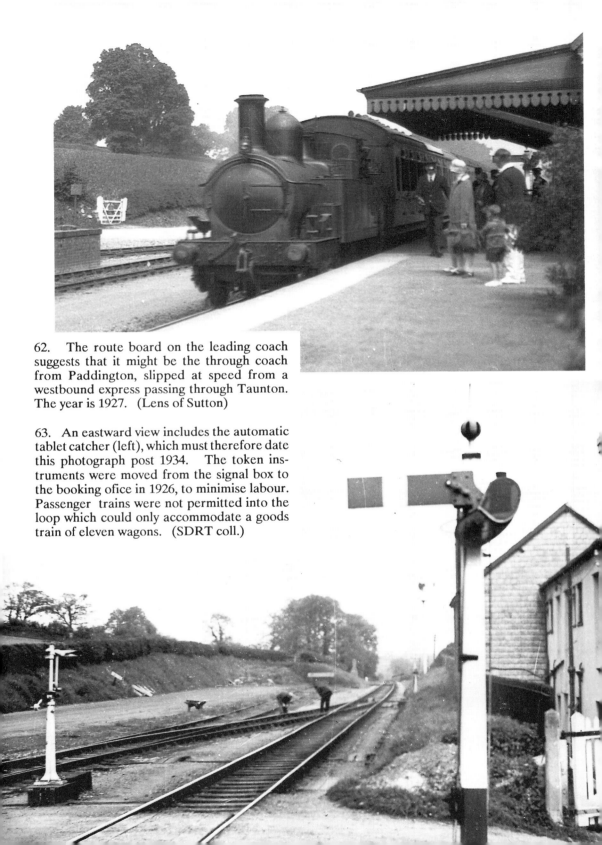

62. The route board on the leading coach suggests that it might be the through coach from Paddington, slipped at speed from a westbound express passing through Taunton. The year is 1927. (Lens of Sutton)

63. An eastward view includes the automatic tablet catcher (left), which must therefore date this photograph post 1934. The token instruments were moved from the signal box to the booking ofice in 1926, to minimise labour. Passenger trains were not permitted into the loop which could only accommodate a goods train of eleven wagons. (SDRT coll.)

64. Cattle traffic to and from the adjacent market and nearby farms formed an important part of railway revenue. Railway staff were required to deal with loading and unloading, cleaning of pens and wagons, and deaths of livestock in transit. (SDRT coll.)

65. The goods yard closed on 6th July 1964 and the shed was demolished soon after. The platform had been lengthened in 1934. Staffing ceased from 21st February 1966. (C.L.Caddy)

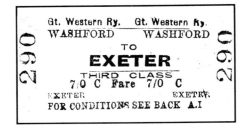

Gt. Western Ry. Gt. Western Ry.
WASHFORD WASHFORD
TO
EXETER
THIRD CLASS
7/0 C Fare 7/0 C
EXETER   EXETER
FOR CONDITIONS SEE BACK A.I

290   290

66. The signal box closed on 24th August 1952, when two ground frames came into use, but luckily the building remained intact. This is the desolate scene in June 1966. (T.Wright)

67. The Somerset & Dorset Railway Trust was formed in 1966 to collate information and collect relics of the S&D. In 1975 it moved its collection of rolling stock from Radstock (see our *Bath to Evercreech Junction* album) to Washford, where work continued on the Trust's main exhibit, 2-8-0 no. 53808. Developments in 1989 included the erection of a new workshop/exhibition building and extension of trackwork, which includes the three-way point from Radstock locomotive depot. (V.Mitchell)

68. The connection with the WSR at the west end passes under level crossing gates recovered from Edington Junction and near to the former Wells goods office. The coach was built by the GWR in 1914 and is used as an office and messroom, the ex-LSWR signal post bearing a backing arm of the type once used at several locations on the SDJR. (V.Mitchell)

69. At the east end of the site, a collection of historic goods vehicles are available for inspection, including this Ruston & Hornsby diesel, once used for shunting at Bath Gasworks. (R.E.Ruffell)

70. The station houses a fine exhibition of S&D relics of great diversity, while the original Washford signal box has been fitted out to represent Midford. The van bears the WSR crest and is used for the transport of permanent way tools and materials. (V.Mitchell)

71. On 11th September 1987, a demonstration loose-coupled goods train was hauled by a class 07 diesel, in readiness for the S&D week-end on the WSR, when no. 53808 returned to steam. The train is on a falling gradient of 1 in 65, just west of Washford. (P.G.Barnes)

BLUE ANCHOR

72.   The loop, down platform (right) and signal box came into use on 5th January 1904. The station was first known as Bradley Gate, the original building (with porch) pre-dating the railway.   (Lens of Sutton)

73.   The down platform building also dates from 1904 and now houses a Great Western Railway Museum.   Note the extensive floral decoration.   (Lens of Sutton)

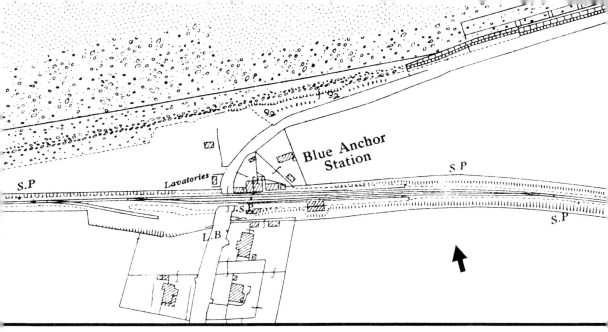

1936 edition, showing the proximity of the
coast.

74. The 1934 extension of the up platform is visible in the distance, as are some of the holiday homes that sprang up in that era bringing further rail traffic. Oil lights and a then modern telephone sign are also to be seen. The shelter on the left was demolished by BR and rebuilt after the re-opening. (Lens of Sutton)

75. A DMU departs for Minehead in June 1965, when the camping coaches had ceased to be watertight and were removed for renovation and transfer to Dawlish Warren. The siding had been opened for goods traffic on 1st April 1913. Conygar Tower is in the background. (T.Wright)

76. The nearest building on the right is the Ladies and has an odd tapered shape due to the proximity of the boundary fence. The tall concrete posts were fitted with pulleys to allow pressurised oil lamps to be hoisted into position. (C.L.Caddy)

Bristol & Exeter Railway.
BLUE ANCHOR
(H)   TO
WATCHET
SECOND CLASS
Watchet   Watchet

363

77. At the far end of the up platform, but barely visible, is a catch point facing towards Washford. It was intended to derail vehicles that had broken loose on the gradient, as the loop points are always set for the up platform until a down train is due. (C.L.Caddy)

78. Named after an inn, the station was over a mile from the nearest village, Carhampton, and was therefore not a source of great revenue. The goods siding was closed on 19th August 1963, three years before this Minehead bound DMU was photographed. (T.Wright)

79. The 17-lever signal box is now unusual in still having a gate wheel. No. 53808 approaches with the 12.00 from Minehead on 16th April 1990. Former camping coaches from Dawlish Warren complete the scene but their track remains disconnected. (V.Mitchell)

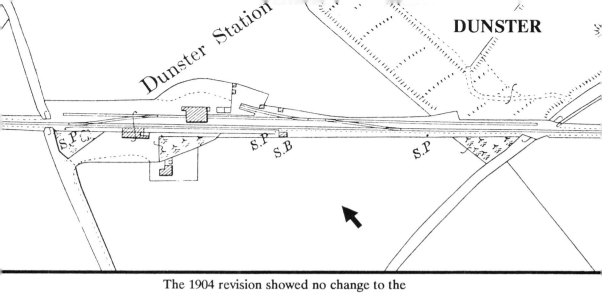

DUNSTER

The 1904 revision showed no change to the
station details, the signal box remaining where
shown until 1934, although having closed on
4th August 1926.

80. The line to Minehead was doubled beyond the level crossing on 19th March 1934. The main goods inward were domestic coal and fertiliser while outwards pit props, agricultural and horticultural products were high on the list. (Lens of Sutton)

81. The yard was congested during the polo season at nearby Dunster Castle, home of one of the directors of the GWR at one period.

Each vehicle is fitted with a comfortable compartment for the groom. (P.Barnfield coll.)

82. Perishable and other urgent goods were often carried in, or attached to, passenger trains, hence the well loaded platform barrow.

No. 6113, a 2-6-2T of the 6100 class, makes its final stop before Minehead in August 1963. (R.E.Toop)

83. The signal box was brought from Maerdy in 1934 to control the new double track to Minehead. It was of standard GWR pattern, with internal staircase. The 11.20 from Minehead passes the oil depot on 31st October 1965. (C.L.Caddy)

84.　In the distance is Sea Lane Crossing,
which was worked by a resident crossing
keeper until closure.　Automatic lights were
brought into use on 28th March 1976.　Goods
services were withdrawn on 6th July 1964.
(C.L.Caddy)

85.   The sidings were being lifted in September 1966, as a Taunton bound DMU runs alongside the footpath linking Sea Lane with the station.   The goods shed was fitted with a 30cwt. capacity crane. (T.Wright)

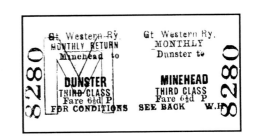

Gt Western Ry.
MONTHLY RETURN
Minehead to

DUNSTER
THIRD CLASS
Fare 6½d P
FOR CONDITIONS

Gt Western Ry.
MONTHLY
Dunster to

MINEHEAD
THIRD CLASS
Fare 6½d P
SEE BACK   W.R

8280   8280

86. From 27th March 1966, the double track was signalled as two single lines and the connections between them at Minehead removed. Most trains used the former up line, even after reopening, but from 1977 the down one was in use and the up was lifted. (C.G.Maggs)

→

88. Similar in design to Washford and Minehead, Dunster had windows similar to the former and a porch as at the latter. Its brick built chimney stacks are, however, distinctive and are seen in 1976. (C.L.Caddy)

87. Only a week after closure in January 1971, an air of despair prevailed but, five years later, trains were running again. In 1980, track was again in place through the goods shed. (C.L.Caddy)

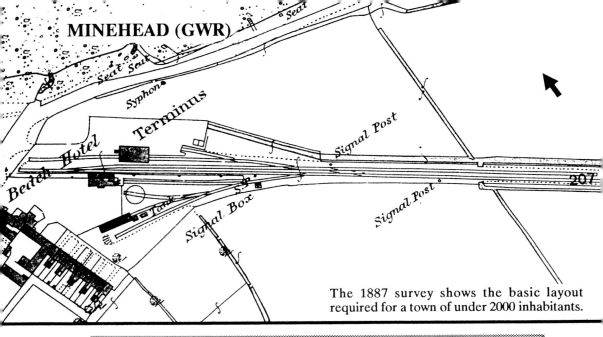

MINEHEAD (GWR)

The 1887 survey shows the basic layout required for a town of under 2000 inhabitants.

89. The terminus served an extensive area westward that included a large part of Exmoor. The four-horse coach nearest to the station may well be the Lynton service which had to negotiate the 1 in 4 Porlock Hill. Note that trains are standing at both platforms. (SDRT coll.)

90. A large perambulator emerges onto platform 2 which was not signalled for passenger trains until 1st July 1905, although there was still no run-round facility provided then. (Lens of Sutton)

The 1904 edition includes an additional siding since the first survey. This was probably used mainly for domestic coal, as the population had increased to around 3000 in that period.

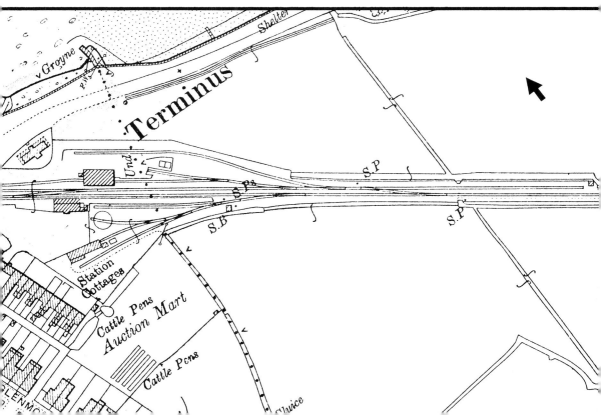

91. This and the next four pictures were taken in 1923 when the population had doubled in ten years to over 6000, creating a strain on railway facilities, particularly at peak holiday periods. Higher Town was still largely undeveloped. (P.Conibeare coll.)

1928

92. To provide additional space due to the rapid development of the town, the GWR erected one of their pagoda-style iron huts with no consideration for aesthetics. No doubt the enamel signs produced a good revenue. This picture shows the signal box located on the short platforms. CL referred to the Cheshire Lines Committee   (P. Conibeare coll.)

1928

93. Viewed from The Esplanade, the station was unimpressive and pedestrians would have had to take care of their footwear after the passage of so many horses. The locomotive shed is on the right. (P.Conibeare coll.)

95. The locomotive shed was moved from Watchet, according to legend, but there is no similarity in photographic evidence. The water tank was of generous capacity. (P. Conibeare coll.)

94. Before even joining the train, passengers were able to discover that Wincarnis could cure brain-fag *and* mental prostration. Those were the days when most of the town's requirements passed through the goods yard gates. (P. Conibeare coll.)

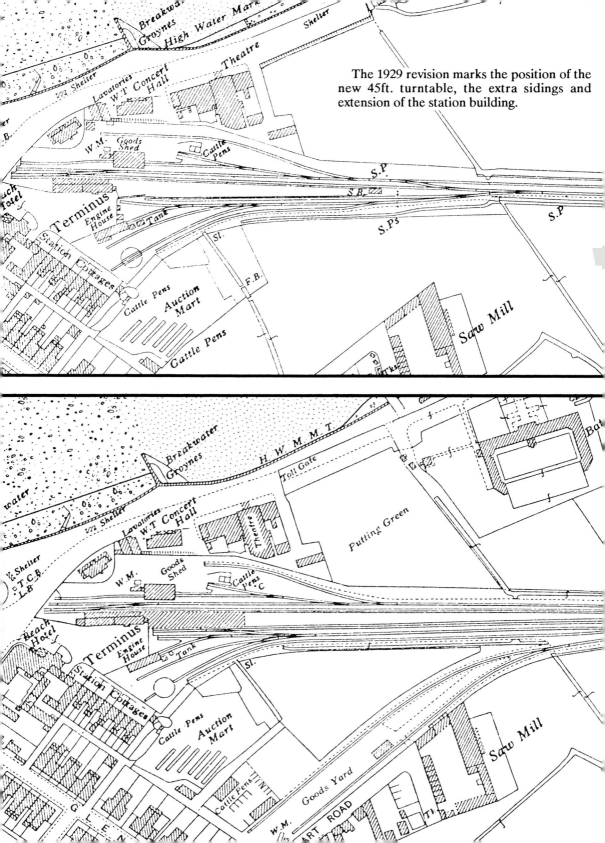

The 1929 revision marks the position of the new 45ft. turntable, the extra sidings and extension of the station building.

The 1936 edition shows the layout at its optimum, with the lengthened platform and new signal box. Some of the new attractions for holidaymakers are also marked. C marks the position of the 6-ton crane.

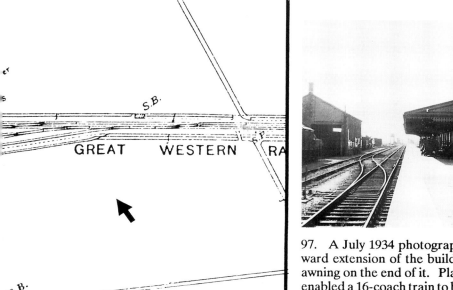

96. The guard's boots gleam as he prepares to blow his whistle, whilst merchandise emerges from a down train. The high-roofed coach bears a roof board and is probably to be attached to a London train at Taunton. Gas lighting has arrived. (P.Barnfield coll.)

97. A July 1934 photograph shows the westward extension of the buildings and the later awning on the end of it. Platform lengthening enabled a 16-coach train to be accommodated. (Mowat coll.)

MINEHEAD (BR)

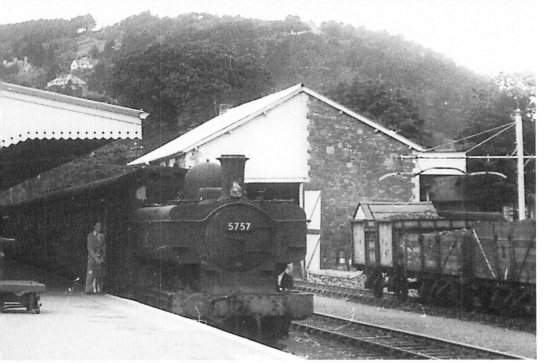

98. When the platforms were lengthened in 1934, a generous canopy was erected, serving both platforms for the first time and also acc-ommodating the full length of most trains, out of season, as witnessed here on 15th July 1958. (H.C.Casserley)

99. The extension was carried out with great care and attention to detail, making the boundary difficult to discern. It is behind the Armstrong Siddeley, elderly when photo-graphed in 1958. (R.M.Casserley)

100. Photographed in 1958, the locomotive shed had not been used since November 1956. Normally only one engine was allocated here - in 1947, it was 0-6-0 no. 2213. (H.C.Casserley)

102. The 1.50pm to Taunton on 4th March 1961 is headed by 5700 class no.9647, while freight is in the care of 2251 class no. 2261. Electric lighting has superseded gas. Although the population had reached 7700, road transport was reducing rail traffic. (E.Wilmshurst)

101. Viewed from near the signal box in about 1959, 5100 class 2-6-2T no. 4128 departs for Taunton. Note that a water column was provided opposite the tank. (C.L.Caddy)

103. The goods yard was still busy in July 1960, as no. 2277 stands ready to depart, having completed its morning shunting. The cattle pens are visible on the right. (R.S.Carpenter)

104. BR standard locomotives were in use in April 1962, no. 82030 being in the process of running round its train. The old order is represented by class 5700 0-6-0PT no. 3789, shunting in the yard, close to the 6-ton crane. (R.E.Toop)

105.   DMUs came into regular use in
September 1962, reducing operating costs and
the frequency of use of the crossover.   The
boundary between the old and new canopies is
clearly seen on 5th September 1965.
(T.Wright)

106.   Aerial passengers view the railway
exhibits at the nearby Butlins Holiday Camp in
September 1965.   They are ex-LBSCR Terrier
no. 78 *Knowle* and ex-LMS no. 6229 *Duchess
of Hamilton.*   (T.Wright)

107. The station is seen in decline on a wet day in September 1965, with weeds rising and the goods shed doors firmly locked. Freight fracilities were withdrawn on 6th July 1964. (T.Wright)

108. Shortly after this photograph was taken, the signals were removed and the box closed. From 27th March 1966, the station was operated as a terminus of two single lines from Dunster, each platform retaining a run-round loop with hand worked points. (C.L.Caddy)

109. The turntable and parachute type water tank were still in place in October 1965 but were removed during the following year, along with the adjacent sidings. The cottages in the background were railway property. (C.L.Caddy)

110. A few mourners turned out in dreary weather on 2nd January 1971, the last day of operation by BR. Note that the main line and the loop had been shortened in 1966. (C.L.Caddy)

MINEHEAD (WSR)

111.   In 1975, the West Somerset Railway signed a 20 year lease of the railway with the owners, the Somerset County Council.   On 28th March 1976, the first train departed for Blue Anchor and this is the scene on 19th May 1981, by which time much of the track had been replaced.
(Alain Lockyer/Somerset Photo News)

112. No. 1163 *Whitehead* arrived on the WSR on 3rd March 1977, having been built by Peckett in 1908. Like many other industrial locomotives it was of limited value on the line. (S.C.Nash)

113. Bearing its BR number (32678) on the smokebox, the Terrier is seen from Minehead platform, on 8th October 1979, having been released from captivity at Butlins. The plan to operate it on the WSR never materialised and it eventually went to work on the Kent & East Sussex Railway. A short history appears in our *Branch Line to Hayling*. (S.C.Nash)

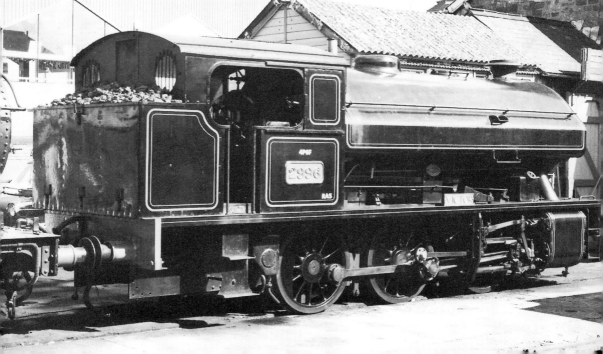

114. Standing at the end of the line on 8th April 1985 is *Vulcan* (left), a Bagnall product, and *Jennifer*, built by Hudswell Clarke & Co. in 1942. Neither are now working on the line. (M.Turvey)

115. *Victor* was built by Bagnalls in 1951 for Margam Steelworks and moved to Austin's Longbridge Works in 1957. It arrived on the WSR in 1975 and worked hard for many years. It now has a less strenuous life on the Strathspey Railway, and was photographed at Minehead in September 1987. (P.G.Barnes)

116. No. 3205 (right) has also served the WSR well since its arrival in March 1987, having claimed a place in history by hauling the first train on the revived Severn Valley Railway on 23rd May 1970. On the left is class 14 diesel no. D9551 while class 4500 no. 5572 was a visitor from Didcot on 10th September 1987. (P.G.Barnes)

117. On 20th June 1989, class 04 no. D2271 was station pilot while ex-SDJR 2-8-0 no.53808 rests in the shed. Amazing feats of restoration have been achieved in this former goods shed. (R.E.Ruffell)

118. Heavy repairs were in progress on 20th June 1989, 0-6-0 no. 3205 being devoid of boiler, while 2-6-2T no. 4561 was being re-assembled, having last run in 1961. It returned to service on 14th October 1989. (R.E.Ruffell)

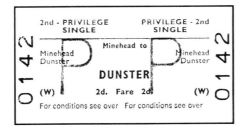

119. On the same day, 2-8-0 no. 53808 was in the shed, while 0-6-0PT no. 6412 stood by the coal heap. This locomotive was built in 1934, withdrawn in 1963 and saw service on the Dart Valley Railway from 1966 until 1976. (R.E.Ruffell)

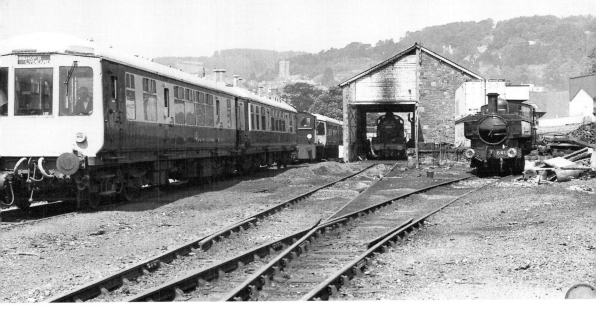

120. The former Maerdy signal box was moved bodily from Dunster on 20th November 1977 and from early 1990 functioned as a ground frame. Plans were announced for a level crossing to be built just beyond it and work was proceeding in early 1990 to fully refit the box; hence the location cupboard on the platform. No. 4561 departs with the last train of the day on 16th April 1990, taking visitors on a journey of scenic delights along one of the premier preserved railways in the country. (V.Mitchell)